19 Lessons in History:

19 Hours of Teaching and Learning Material for Parents, Guardians and Teachers of High School Students and Key Stage 3 Students

BY

Robin Walker

REKLAW EDUCATION LTD
London (U.K.)

19 Lessons in Black History

CONTENTS

OPENING REMARKS: HOW TO USE THIS BOOK

This book is aimed at parents and teachers who would like information to teach their children Black History.

The material was designed to be used for children at around Key Stage 3 Level – i.e. young people aged 11 to 14. The lessons can work with slightly older or younger people. I, myself, have profitably used this material with adults. However, in quoting the sources, it was often necessary to simplify the wording to make it accessible to the target age group.

The first ten lessons concern **Ancient and Mediaeval Africa**. The first five classes deal with different African civilisations. The second five classes deal with early African contributions to science and technology. The last nine lessons concern **Black People in the Atlantic Age** (i.e. since the time of Christopher Columbus). These classes deal with the Atlantic Slave Trade and Black Resistance to it. It also covers Black personalities in British history, such as Olaudah Equiano. The final part of the book is an **Image Bank** to supplement the information in the lessons.

Parents should be aware that each lesson lasts about one hour in length and may be structured like this.
   (1) The students should WRITE the **Lesson Title** and the **Aim of Lesson** into their note book or on a sheet of paper. This should take about **one minute**.
   (2) The parent or teacher should READ and DISCUSS the material and the sources WITH the students. The students should STUDY the maps and the relevant illustrations from the **Image Bank** as well. One strategy is to ask the students to take turns in reading a sentence each. The reading and the discussion should take about **fifteen to twenty minutes** in total.
   (3) The students should WRITE written answers to the **Activity** questions in their note book or on the sheet of paper. This should take most of the remaining **forty or so minutes**. They do not need to copy out the questions unless the activity specifically asks them to, but they must write answers in full sentences.
   (4) The parent or teacher should CHECK over the answers with the students in the last **five minutes**.
   (5) If any students finish early, get them to sketch something relevant from the **Image Bank** into their notebooks.

Teachers who are reading this will, of course, be able to come up with more inventive ways to work through these lessons.

Robin Walker

LESSON ONE: THE NILE VALLEY

Aim of Lesson: To introduce the controversy surrounding Ancient Egypt

The Nile River flowed from Uganda to the Mediterranean. The oldest civilisations on earth emerged there. The most important of these was Ancient Egypt. It lasted for thousands of years. (See also **Image Bank** Figures 1 and 2).

Not all historians agree on how old Egypt was. Some writers think its first kings ruled about 3000 BC. Other writers say they ruled before 5000 BC. Pharaoh Mena was the first king of Egypt. Historians date him to anywhere between 5867 BC and 2789 BC (See **Source A**). The history of Ancient Egypt covers the rise and fall of Thirty Dynasties of rulers. Most historians agree that the last dynasty fell in 343 BC.

Egypt is in Africa but that does not prove that the Ancient Egyptians were Africans. After all, Egypt today is only about one third African. Most of the Modern Egyptians are Arabians or Europeans. The Europeans conquered Egypt from Greece in 332 BC. The Arabians conquered Egypt from the Middle East in 639 AD. These conquerors have become the majority of the population. The Ancient Egyptian period was much older than this. So who were the ancient Egyptians?

In January 1974, UNESCO (United Nations Educational, Scientific and Cultural Organisation) held a debate to discuss the people of Ancient Egypt. At the debate, two African scholars, Professor Diop and Professor Obenga, presented the evidence that the Ancient Egyptians were Africans. 18 European and Arab scholars presented evidence that they were Europeans. The two African scholars won the argument over the 18 opponents.

Source A

This table shows the dates (BC) for the first kings of Dynasties 1, 6, 12, and 18. Historians do not agree on these dates. Most textbooks use dates that are similar to those given Meyer (writing in 1887) and Breasted (1906).

HISTORIAN	DYNASTIES			
	I	VI	XII	XVIII
Manetho (241 BC)	5717	4426	3440	1674
Champollion-Figeac (1839)	5867	4426	3703	1822
Brugsch (1877)	4400	3300	2466	1700
Meyer (1887)	3180	2530	2130	1530
Breasted (1906)	3400	2625	2000	1580
Petrie (1929)	4553	3282	2586	1587
MacNaughton (1932)	5776	4360	3389	1709
Pochan (1971)	5619	4326	3336	1595
Rohl (1998)	2789	2224	1800	1193
Chinweizu (1999)	4443	3162	1994	1788
Walker (2006)	5660	4402	3405	1709

(Robin Walker, *When We Ruled*, 2006)

This is the conclusion of the UNESCO debate

Although Unesco sent each of the Egyptologists details of what we wanted to discuss, not all of the speakers had prepared research as good as the painstakingly researched work of Professors Diop and Obenga.

(G. Mokhtar, *Annex to Chapter 1: Report of the symposium on The Peopling of Ancient Egypt*, in *UNESCO General History of Africa, Volume 2*, 1990)

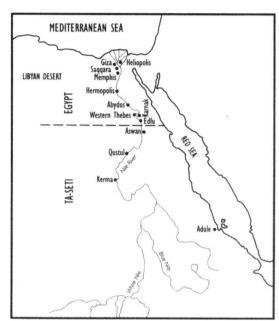

Map of Ancient Egypt and Ta-Seti.

ACTIVITIES . . .

1a. Where did the oldest civilisations emerge?

1b. Why do you think that civlisations usually emerge near to a river?

2a. How long have Europeans and Arabians lived in Egypt? Work it out!

2b. Were either groups living there before 343 BC?

3. In your own words, what happened at the UNESCO debate?

4. Study **Source A.** Manetho was an Ancient Egyptian historian who wrote about Egypt in 241 BC. Some historians agree with his information, give or take a hundred or so years, but others do not believe him. Make two lists of historians and when they were writing by copying out and completing the table.

Historians that agree with Manetho	Historians that disagree with Manetho
Champollion-Figeac (1839) *MacNaughton (1932)*	*Brugsch (1877)*

7

LESSON TWO: THE SONGHAI EMPIRE

Aim of Lesson: To study the West African empire of Songhai

The Songhai Empire was in West Africa. It had a long history going back to 690 AD. The great period was from 1469 to 1591. During this period, the empire became one of the largest states on earth. It was nearly the same size as all the European countries combined. Its population was 50 million people. This is more than that of Black America today. It was a very urban society and had 400 cities. The empire controlled two-thirds of the trade of West Africa. It had huge resources of gold, salt and copper.

Sunni Ali (ruled 1464-1492) founded the empire. From his capital city of Gao, his armies conquered many parts of West Africa. In the sixteenth century, the empire controlled the regions now called Senegal, Gambia, Guinea, Mauritania, Mali, Northern Nigeria and Niger. Goods were on sale all over the empire. These included gold, copper, salt, leather, cotton and books. It was wealthy empire. A common saying at the time was: "Against poverty, take a trip to West Africa."

Most of our detailed information on the empire came from two great history books. In 1656, Abdurrahman Al-Sadi, an African historian, wrote *History of the Sudan*. He was head of one of the Songhai universities. In 1526, a Moroccan historian called Leo Africanus visited the Songhai city of Timbuktu. He wrote *A History and Description of Africa*. (See also **Image Bank** Figure 3).

In 1591, the empire collapsed. The Arabs of Morocco invaded the country. The invading army was armed with guns and cannons made in England. After the invasion, the Europeans intensified the slave trade against Africans.

Source A

I saw the ruin and collapse of the science of history. I saw that its gold pieces and small change were both disappearing. This science is rich in gems and can give many lessons because it gives people knowledge of their country, their ancestors, their records, the names of their heroes and their biographies. With the help of God I began to write about all that I was able to find out about the princes of the Songhai people. I wrote about their adventures, history, exploits and battles. Then I added the history of Timbuktu from the foundation of that city, of the princes that ruled there, and also the scholars and saints who lived there.

(Abdurrahman Al-Sadi, *History of the Sudan,* 1656)

Source B

In Timbuktu there are lots of judges, doctors and clerics all receiving good salaries from the King. He pays great respect to men of learning. There is a big demand for books in manuscript, imported from North Africa. More profit is made from the book trade than from any other line of business.

(Leo Africanus, *A History and Description of Africa,* 1526)

8

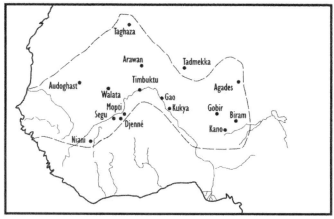

Map of the Songhai Empire.

ACTIVITIES . . .

1. Copy and compete the following information.

The _____ _____ had a long history. Its history dated back to _____ AD. The great period dated from _____ to _____ . It had _____ cities. The capital city was called _____. Most of the information on it comes from _____ books. One was called _____ _____ _____ _____. The other was called A History and Description of _____. The founder of the empire was _____ _____.

690	Songhai Empire	1469	History of the Sudan	Gao
2	Africa	1591	Sunni Ali	400

2. List four modern countries that were part of the Songhai Empire in the 16th century.

3a. Who was Abdurrahman Al-Sadi?

3b. Why was he important?

4. What happened in 1591?

5. According to **Source A,** why is it important to study history?

6. According to **Source B,** what was the biggest selling product in Timbuktu?

EXTENDED WRITING

Write a newspaper report on the Songhai Empire for the *Financial Times.* Say why British readers should be interested in visiting the empire for business reasons and for educational reasons.

Begin like this: *The Songhai Empire is very wealthy. There are lots of business opportunities to invest and make money in. Among these are . . .*
Mention the wealth, population, resources, businesses, education and sources for more information.

LESSON THREE: MEDIAEVAL NIGERIA

Aim of Lesson: To study the mediaeval kingdoms of Southern Nigeria
In the mediaeval period, Nigeria had two great civilisations. There was the Yoruba Kingdoms, and also the Benin Empire. Both peoples produced some of the very best metal art in the world. (See also **Image Bank** Figures 4, 6 and 9).

The Yoruba Kingdoms existed from 600 AD to about 1500 AD. The Yorubas had city-states that had 150,000 to 250,000 inhabitants. Art objects of the highest quality were found in their ruins. Among these were glazed urns, ceramic tiles with pictures of animals and gods on them. There were also bronze implements and gigantic granite figures. The Yorubas introduced the growing of yams, the making of cheese and the breeding of horses into West Africa. They had brilliant metal working artists. They had gold-casters, cotton-weavers, wood-carvers and potters. The capital city was called Ile-Ife. Glass was produced there from the beginning of the city. In around 1100 AD, Queen Oluwo had the city paved.

The Benin Empire began as a kingdom in around 900 AD. In 1473, it became an empire. Its capital city was very impressive. In 1283, the first walls and moats were built. In 1460, the innermost walls were built and had nine gates. This part contained the palaces. Also there were the houses of the nobility and workshops for the skilled workers. They had unions of ivory carvers, iron and brass smiths, weavers and embroiders, drummers and sculptors. Surrounding this area was the outer city. The whole thing was built on a horizontal vertical grid. One archaeologist said that the building work was as large as the Great Wall of China.

When the Slave Trade was at its height, the Yoruba states suffered greatly. It lost many people. The Benin Empire lasted until 1897. That year the British army invaded and conquered their land.

Source A
The kind of evidence field archaeologists like is the pavement of Ile-Ife, a former Yoruba capital. This was decorated by corncobs over its surface before firing. One archaeologist, who had seen it assured me that the corncobs were from America. Ife was paved about A.D. 1100 or earlier. If so, this site provides the evidence that archaeologists want for American plants in Africa before Columbus sailed to America.
(David Kelley quoted in Ivan Van Sertima, *Early America Revisited*, 1998)

Source B
The largest clay construction in the world before modern times was Benin City in the Mid Western state of Nigeria. Modern European scholars first reported them in 1903. In April 1967 Mr Patrick Darling found that the total length of the earthworks was probably between 5,000 and 8,000 miles. The total amount of earth moved was from 380-460 million m³.
(Norris & Ross McWhirter, *Guinness Book of Records, 21st Edition*, October 1974)

Map of Mediaeval Nigeria.

ACTIVITIES . . .

1a. What things did the Yorubas introduce into West Africa that were not there before?

1b. What sort of things did they make?

1c. Why was Queen Oluwo important?

2. Make a time line of the main events in Benin from 900 to 1897.

3a. Study **Source A.** What was used to decorate the pavements?

3b. Where did it come from?

3c. At what date did it get there?

3d. How do you think it got there and why is this important? (HINT – Christopher Columbus was supposed to have discovered America in 1492!)

4a Study **Source B.** Give the name of the source?

4b. What was important about Benin City?

LESSON FOUR: THE EAST AFRICAN COAST

Aim of Lesson: To study the ancient history of the Swahili Civilisation

The Swahili Confederation consisted of a number of major cities on the East African coast. They existed between the eighth and the sixteenth centuries. They had wonderful architecture. Their mosques were as grand as the cathedrals of Europe. The legendary adventures of Sinbad the Sailor took place there. Even in ruin these sites are tourist attractions in Kenya and Tanzania. Among the ruins were indoor toilets, piped water and drains. (See also **Image Bank** Figures 7 and 10).

The various cities were spread over 2500 miles from Somalia to Mozambique. The major city-states were Mogadishu and Brava in Somalia, Lamu, Mombassa and Malindi in Kenya, Kilwa off the coast of Tanzania, and finally Sofala in Mozambique. There was another major city in Mozambique called Sinna. The ruins of more than 50 other Swahili towns and cities have been found.

Ibn Battuta was a Moroccan traveller. In 1331, he visited the East African cities. He liked Mogadishu. He wrote that it was a city "endless in its size." He also described their food. They fed him rice, yoghurt, boiled green banana and mangoes. From there he sailed on to Mombassa and then to Kilwa. In 1353, his *Travels in Asia and Africa* was completed. Duarte Barbosa was Portuguese. He described the East African coast in 1500. His writings were completed in 1517.

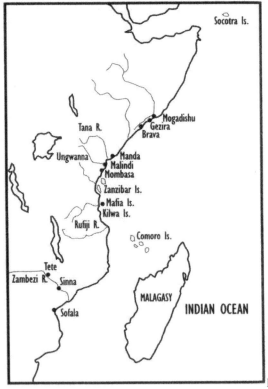

Map of the East African Coast.

12

Source A

We spent a night on the island of Mombassa, and then set sail for Kilwa. It was the principal city on the coast. Most of its inhabitants were of very black complexion. They have tattoo marks on their faces, like some West Africans. Kilwa is one of the most beautiful and well-constructed cities in the world. The whole of it is elegantly built.

(Ibn Battuta, *Travels in Asia and Africa*, 1353)

Source B

The people of the coast are finely dressed. They wear many rich garments of gold, silk and cotton. They also wear a lot of gold and silver chains and bracelets, which they wear on their legs and arms. They wear many jewelled earrings in their ears.

(Duarte Barbosa, *The Book of Duarte Barbosa*, 1517)

Source C

This source describes the actions of Portuguese captains da Gama, Ravasio, Almeida, Saldanha, Soares and D'Acunha in East Africa.

Back again on the coast in 1502, this time with a number of ships ... da Gama threatens to burn Kilwa unless its ruler will acknowledge the supremacy of the king of Portugal and pay him yearly tribute in gold. Ravasio does the same at Zanzibar and Brava. Meeting resistance, Almeida storms Kilwa and Mombasa, burning and destroying. Saldanha ravages Berbera. Soares destroys Zeila. D'Acunha attacks Brava.

(Basil Davidson, *Old Africa Rediscovered*, 1959)

ACTIVITIES . . .

1a. List 4 facts about the Swahili Confederation.

1b. In your opinion, what was the most important fact and why?

2. Match the Heads to the Tails

HEADS	TAILS
Brava was in	Mozambique
Mombasa was in	Tanzania
Kilwa was in	Kenya
Sinna was in	Somalia

3. According to **Source A,** what was important about the city of Kilwa?

4. According to **Source B,** how did the people of East Africa dress? Is there anything here that tells us how wealthy the people were?

EXTENDED WRITING

Write a newspaper article called *The Portuguese Storm The Coast.* Describe the events that happened as if you were there.

LESSON FIVE: ANCIENT AXUM

Aim of Lesson: To study the ancient history of Ethiopia and Eritrea

Ethiopia and Eritrea have very long histories. Although they are separate countries today, they were one kingdom in the ancient world. The capital city of their kingdom was called Axum. The country was also called Axum. Trade goods passed through this city to a port on the Red Sea coast called Adule. The first great king of the empire was called Zoscales. He lived in about 50 AD.

Ethiopian and Eritrean ships sailed to Iran, Arabia, India, and Byzantium (Turkey). They shipped cargoes of gold and ivory to these places. In return they bought silk cloth, cotton, swords and glass cups. Out of the gold, they made statues. Some of these were a staggering 15 feet tall. They made steel weapons, pottery, and olive oil. They also minted their own gold and silver coins.

In 330 AD, Emperor Ezana made the country Christian. It was one of the oldest surviving Christian nations in the world. He also introduced new written scripts such as the Ethiopic. He also built a castle complex, the Cathedral of Saint Mary of Zion, several other churches, and also convents. (See also **Image Bank** Figures 5 and 17).

Coin of an Axumite ruler. (Photo: Classical Numismatic Group, Inc.)

Source A
One great feature of the Axum kingdom was its coinage. Almost no other country anywhere in the world could afford to make gold coins. The only other countries that had gold coins were Rome, Persia, and India.
(Stuart C. Munro-Hay, *Axum Coinage*, in *African Zion*, 1993)

Source B
Soon after its creation, the Ethiopic script began to influence the scripts of Armenia and Georgia [i.e. in Southern Russia].
(Fari Supiya, *Ethiopia's First Christian Emperor: Ezana of Axum*, in *West Africa, Issue 4303*)

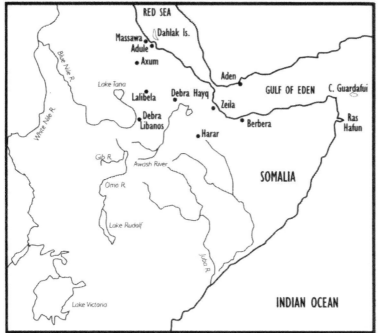

Map of Axum.

ACTIVITIES . . .

1. Match the Heads to the Tails

HEADS	**TAILS**
Ethiopia and Eritrea were called	Zoscales
The main port was on the	Adule
The port was called	Red Sea
The first great king was called	Axum

2a. What goods did the Axumites sell to the outside world?

2b. What things did they make?

2c. What goods did they buy from the outside world?

2d What countries did these goods come from?

3. Why was Emperor Ezana such an important figure?

4. According to **Source A,** what was so important about the Axumites making gold coins?

5. According to **Source B,** why was the Ethiopic script so important?

LESSON SIX: ASTRONOMY

Aim of Lesson: To study early African contributions to astronomy

The Ancient Egyptians made great discoveries in astronomy. They gave names to 43 of the star constellations. They also invented the solar zodiac. By 4241 BC, some say earlier, they invented the solar calendar. This is the calendar that we use today. It has 365.25 days. They began each year by observing the rising of a bright star called Sirius.

In the Songhai Empire, astronomy was studied at Timbuktu. They used it to layout buildings, such as mosques. The Dogon, for example, one of the old Songhai peoples, held on to a remarkable tradition of astronomy. Their tradition dates from the early 1300s. Their scholars had accurately described the rings of Saturn, some of the moons of Jupiter, the spiral structure of the Milky Way Galaxy and the surface of the moon. They also studied the sixty-year synchronisation of the orbits of Jupiter and Saturn. They also studied the existence of companion stars affecting the movement of Sirius, the brightest star.

The Dogon were the first to discover the existence of Sirius B, one of the companion stars orbiting Sirius. They correctly describe it as a white dwarf and say it is the densest type of star in the universe. They also describe the fifty-year orbit of Sirius C, another companion star around Sirius.

Ethiopia has a number of mediaeval manuscripts that contain astronomical information. Some of them show knowledge of five planets: Mercury, Venus, Mars, Saturn and Jupiter. Other manuscripts mention solar eclipses in 1241 AD, 1528 and 1727. A manuscript mentions a lunar eclipse in 1620. An Ethiopian (and also a Chinese) manuscript recorded the appearance of a nova in 1618.

Source A

Other Timbuktu manuscripts dating back 600 years include beautifully drawn diagrams of the orbits of planets, which demonstrate the use of complex mathematical calculations. There are also recordings of astronomical events, including a meteor shower in August 1583.

(Curtis Abraham, *Stars of the Sahara,* in *New Scientist,* 2007)

Source B

The appearance of comets shocked Europeans of the Middle Ages. In Timbuktu, their scholars wrote about it as a matter of scientific interest. Earthquakes and eclipses were also things that scholars were interested in.

(Lady Lugard, *A Tropical Dependency*, 1905)

Source C

The Dogon deserve credit for having discovered Sirius B and the white dwarf as a category of star.

(Charles Finch, *The Star of Deep Beginnings*, 1991)

Old Swahili astronomical texts from the Jumba La Mtwana Museum, Kenya (Photo: Robin Walker).

ACTIVITIES . . .

1. What contributions did the Ancient Egyptians make to astronomy?

2. List 5 things that indicate the astronomical knowledge of the Songhai (including the Dogon).

3. What astronomical information is in the old Ethiopian manuscripts?

4. According to **Sources A** and **B,** what sort of things did the astronomers and scholars of Timbuktu write about?

5. According to **Source C,** what two things did the Dogon discover?

EXTENDED WRITING

Write two diary entries on seeing a comet on 12 April 1514. Write one article from Timbuktu and the other one from London. In Timbuktu, they would have known that comets are naturally occurring scientific facts. In London, it would have been seen as a bad omen!

LESSON SEVEN: NAVIGATION

Aim of Lesson: Did Malians get to Central America before Columbus?

In 1342, an Arab scholar wrote a book called *Masalik ab Absar*. In the tenth chapter of this book, there is an account of two large shipping voyages ordered by a West African king in 1311. The book does not name the king but modern writers identify him as Mansa (i.e. Emperor) Abubakari II. He ruled a West African empire called Mali. Mali was the dominant power in West Africa before the Songhai Empire in **Lesson Two**. (See also **Image Bank** Figure 12).

According to the book, this king sent 200 ships filled with men and a further 200 ships stocked with food, gold and water to last for two years. The ruler sent them on a mission to discover the extremity of the Atlantic Ocean. In time, one ship returned. Its captain told the Malian ruler of his adventures. "Prince," he said, "we sailed for a long time, up to the moment when we encountered in mid-ocean a violent current. My ship was last. The others sailed on, and gradually each of them entered this place, they disappeared and did not come back. We did not know what had happened to them. As for me, I returned to where I was and did not enter the current."

The ruler decided to see for himself. He had 2000 ships prepared, 1000 of which had food. They set sail across the Atlantic. Where did they end up?

This all suggests that Malians visited the Americas in 1311. This was 181 years before Christopher Columbus "discovered" this continent. There is other evidence

- Christopher Columbus said that he acquired metal goods of West African manufacture from the Native Americans
- Two Negro skeletons from this period were found in the Caribbean
- An inscription in an old African script was found
- The Native Americans made fourteenth century carvings that show Africans

Source A

The Indians brought me handkerchiefs of cotton that were symmetrically woven. They were in colours like those I saw in Sierra Leone and Guinea with no differences.
(Christopher Columbus, *Journal of the Third Voyage*, 1498)

Source B

The presence of Negroes in America before Columbus is proved by the representation of Negroes in early American sculpture. It is also proved by Columbus who said that Negro traders from West Africa sold a gold alloy of precisely the same type as those he saw in America.
(Leo Wiener, *Africa and the Discovery of America, Volume III*, 1922)

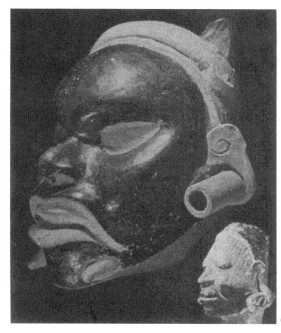

Carving made in Mexico: 14th Century.

ACTIVITIES . . .

1. Match the Heads to the Tails

HEADS	TAILS
In 1342, an Arab scholar	ended up in Central America
The book	wrote a book
Modern scholars think	mentions an event in 1311
Mansa [i.e. Emperor] Abubakari II	the king was called Mansa Abubakari II
The voyage probably	sent his sailors on a voyage

2. For what reasons did they stock half of the ships with food, gold and water?

3. In each case, explain how each of the four pieces of evidence suggests that Africans had got to Central America before Columbus.

4a. According to **Source A,** what did the Indians (i.e. Native Americans) bring to Columbus?

4b. What does it prove?

5. **Source B** was published in 1922. When it was published, people did not believe Leo Wiener. Why do you think this was?

LESSON EIGHT: METALLURGY

Aim of Lesson: To study early African contributions to metallurgy

In the Nigeria region, the Igbos made great developments in metallurgy. In the ninth century, Igbo craftsmen made splendid pieces from leaded bronze. In royal burials archaeologists found fine copper chains, bracelets, staff ornaments, vessels made in the shape of sea shells, drinking cups, pots, sword scabbards, an altar stand, pendants and fly whisks – a symbol of royal power. (See also **Image Bank** Figures 4, 8 and 9).

The artefacts were made of copper or from leaded bronze. Leaded bronze is an alloy of copper, tin, silver and lead. The artefacts were made using a six stage manufacturing process called the Lost Wax technique ... as follows:
1. Make a rough clay model of the product about to be made. The model must be the same size as the finished product
2. Go over the clay model with all the intricate details that the finished product is going to have with 3 millimetre thickness of beeswax
3. Go over the beeswax with a second layer of clay covering the wax
4. Fire everything in a kiln. The melting point of beeswax is lower than that of clay. They beeswax melts and runs out leaving a 3 millimetre gap
5. Melt the copper, tin, silver and lead. Pour these molten metals into the 3 millimetre gap left by the wax
6. Wait for every thing to cool. The liquid metal will now become a solid. Break off the outer and the inner layers of clay. What is left is the finished product made of metal.

At a later date, the Yoruba and the Benin civilisations made use of this technique. The technique is still used today. It is used to make car parts.

In East Africa, steel smelting has been going on since 500 AD. Steel is iron that has been made with extra carbon added. This makes the iron much harder. Steel smelters were found in Tanzania that had blowpipes and bellows to raise the heat.

The East Africans produced steel using the most sophisticated technique the world had ever seen before the nineteenth century. For hundreds of years, the Swahilis traded this steel across the Indian Ocean to Arabia, India and China.

Source A

Two University professors found something of great interest to those interested in the history of technology. Peter Schmidt and Donald Avery found that as long as 2,000 years ago Africans in Tanzania had produced carbon steel. They made the steel in preheated forced draft furnaces. This method was technologically more sophisticated than any developed in Europe until the mid-nineteenth century.

(Debra Shore, *Steel-Making in Ancient Africa,* in *Blacks in Science,* 1983)

The superb workmanship of the Igbo artefacts make them a wonder to behold.

(Laure Meyer, *Art and Craft in Africa,* 1995)

ACTIVITIES . . .

1. Copy and compete the following information.

The _____ of _____ made great developments in metallurgy. They made products from _____ or _____ _____. They made goods using the _____ _____ technique called _____ _____. In East Africa _____ was being made as early as _____ _____.

Nigeria	leaded bronze	500 AD	lost wax
six stage	Igbo	steel	copper

2a. What is the lost wax technique?

2b. Apart from the Igbo Civilisation, who else used the technique? What did they use it to make?

3. What is steel?

4. According to **Source A,** what was special about the making of East African steel?

5. What did the author of **Source B** think of the Igbo artefacts?

EXTENDED WRITING

Write an article for a science magazine called "Bronze and Steel in Early Africa". Mention:
- The Igbo artefacts of the ninth century
- The Lost Wax Technique
- Steel smelting in East Africa
- Say why scientists should be interested in this information

LESSON NINE: ARCHITECTURE

Aim of Lesson: To introduce historical architecture in Africa

There are eyewitness records of old African monuments. In Ghana, the city of Kumasi was a great place. In 1874, one visitor to the city wrote the following:

"A prisoner showed me the sights of Kumasi. We went to the king's palace, which consists of many courtyards ... Each had two gates or doors, so that each yard was a thoroughfare. The doors here had padlocks. There were ten or twelve courtyards. The part of the palace fronting the street was made of stone and had the same style as Moroccan houses. It had suites of apartments on the first floor. The rooms upstairs remind me of Wardour Street in Central London. Each was a perfect Old Curiosity Shop. Books in many languages, glass, clocks, silver plate, old furniture, Persian rugs, Kidderminster carpets, pictures and engravings ..."

Unfortunately, this building is no longer standing. The British destroyed it in 1896. Of the buildings that are still standing are

- The Grand Mosque of Djenné
- The Great Mosque of Kilwa
- The Church of St George in Lalibela

The Grand Mosque in the Malian city of Djenné is the largest clay brick building in the world. It is the finest example of medieval Western Sudanic architecture. Koy Konboro, the 26th king of Djenné, built it in 1204 AD. After converting to Islam, Konboro dismantled his palace and had a mosque built on the same site. The Grand Mosque is roughly square. Each side is 56 metres in length. The total area is the same size as three football pitches. Each side faces north, south, east or west. It has three towers on one side, each with projecting wooden buttresses typical of the Western Sudanic style. The monument resembles a castle.

In Great Mosque in the Tanzanian city of Kilwa, was once the largest of the Swahili temples. It was founded in the tenth or eleventh century. They enlarged it in the thirteenth and fifteenth centuries. The north prayer hall was built first. The domed extension, to the south, was built later. Its roof is complicated. It is partly domed and partly barrel shaped. The interior has octagonal shaped columns. (See **Image Bank** Figure 10).

The Ethiopian city of Lalibela replaced Axum as the capital city. Emperor Lalibela (1150-1220 AD) dreamt of creating a New Jerusalem as his capital. He chose a mountainous site far to the south of Axum. There, he built 11 churches. All were carved out of solid rock by hammer and chisel to an astonishing level of mathematical precision. The most famous of the Lalibela churches is the House of Saint George. From the top of the monument, looking downwards, the Church is in the shape of a concentric cross. It is more than 12 metres deep. The outer wall of the church seems to show 4 storeys. Many writers consider the city the Eighth Wonder of the World. (See **Image Bank** Figure 11).

The Grand Mosque of Djenné. (Photo: Copyright Musée de l'Homme, Paris, Armée de l'Air).

ACTIVITIES . . .

1. Sketch the three monuments.

2. How large was the Grand Mosque of Djenné?

3. What was complicated about the building of the Great Mosque of Kilwa?

4a. Explain in some detail how was the Church of St George was built?

4b. Do you think it was the Eighth Wonder of the World? Give reasons for your point of view.

LESSON TEN: MEDICINE

Aim of Lesson: To study ancient medicine and surgery from Africa

The Ancient Egyptians invented scientific medicine. They wrote the first medical textbooks in the world. One of these is now called the Edwin Smith Surgical Papyrus. The scroll describes 48 examples of head and neck surgery. Another famous manuscript was the Ebers Papyrus.

The Egyptians also started the diagnostic method. This is where . . .
1. The patient would describe the symptoms to the doctor.
2. The doctor then looks over the patient.
3. The patient would provide a urine sample.
4. The doctor would take the pulse.
5. The doctor would give a course of treatment.

During the period of the Songhai Empire, West Africans made great advances in medicine. Surgery was one of the subjects taught at the University of Djenné. They performed eye cataract operations. Sunni Ali, the great Songhai ruler, was mummified after his death. This shows that they had good knowledge of human anatomy. Finally, the Songhai used soap. It was locally manufactured.

West African countries used a large range of plants, minerals and animal material for medical purposes. They used local anaesthetics and had treatments for asthma, bronchitis, diabetes, malaria, muscular-skeletal pain and scurvy. They used plants that had treated sickle cell and other plants that repelled insects.

Inoculation for smallpox, the forerunner of vaccination, has had a long history. West Africans invented many smallpox inoculation techniques before the Europeans. They also quarantined ill patients to protect the rest of the community from infection. Enslaved Africans introduced such vaccines into America.

Ethiopia possesses a small but important number of medical manuscripts. They describe treatments for epilepsy, fever, syphilis, rabies, skin diseases, kidney problems, haemorrhoids, constipation, diarrhoea, itching, coughing, sterility and even snoring. In the case of rabies, Ethiopian manuscripts mention that a bite from a rabid dog could kill. Other manuscripts show that the Ethiopians knew the incubation period for rabies was 40 days.

Source A
This shows how medicine was organised in the Songhai Empire
A family practised a single branch of medicine on a hereditary basis. One family was specialised in the eyes, the stomach, and so on.
(Cheikh Anta Diop, Precolonial Black Africa, 1959)

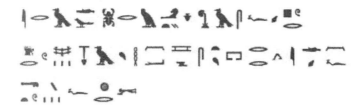

Translation: *"The weakness of the heart is from a tumor all the way to the lung and liver. The patient grows deaf as his vessels have collapsed"*

(*The Ebers Papyrus,* 1674 BC)

Source C
Mather, Colman and Colden were all slave owners. They all gathered the impression from their slaves that inoculation was nearly universal in Africa at the time that African slaves had left Africa.

(Eugenia Herbert, *Smallpox Inoculation in Africa,* in *Journal of African History,* 1975)

ACTIVITIES . . .

1. What information was in the Edwin Smith Papyrus?

2. In your own words, what was the diagnostic method?

3. List 5 things that indicate the medical knowledge of the Songhai.

4. What medical information is in old Ethiopian manuscripts?

5. According to **Source A,** how was medicine organised in the Songhai Empire? How is this similar to or different from how it is organised in modern Britain?

6. Study **Source B.** List the anatomical terms mentioned.

7. Mather, Coleman and Colden were slave owners. According to **Source C,** what did their enslaved Africans tell them?

EXTENDED WRITING

Write a review of *Ancient and Mediaeval Africa.* In 5 paragraphs describe:
- Two of the ancient kingdoms
- The voyage to America
- The African contributions to architecture
- The African contribution to medicine and surgery

LESSON ELEVEN: ENSLAVEMENT

Aim of lesson: to study the link between the enslavement of Africans and the Atlantic Age

The Atlantic Age began in the fifteenth century. During this period, the European nations of Spain and Portugal made important voyages across the Atlantic Ocean to the Americas. These voyages changed the global balance of power.

This began a sad chapter for the history of Africans. This began an equally sad chapter for the history of the Native people of the Americas.

The Spanish and Portuguese killed the Native Americans and took their land. They mass enslaved Africans. Race relations in Europe also changed. There were 3 million Africans living in Spain and Portugal in 1492. They were forced to leave. Many were killed.

The mass enslavement of Africans began in 1441. A Portuguese sailor started it by kidnapping twelve Africans from the coast of Morocco. On his return he gave the Africans to Prince Henry of Portugal. The Prince met with Pope Martin V to tell him of his plans for more conquests and enslavement. The Pope offered to grant "to all of those who shall be engaged in the said war, complete forgiveness of all their sins."

In 1482 the Portuguese built Elmina Castle on the coast of Ghana. It was the first of many dungeons to hold captured Africans awaiting the next slave ship. The local ruler, Kwame Ansa, opposed the building of the dungeon but was forced to back down. The Portuguese burnt his village. At a later date, dungeons were built all along the West African coast.

After Christopher Columbus arrived in the Americas in 1492, his people began the war against the Native Americans (the so-called 'Indians'). As the Native Americans were killed off, Europeans took over their land. Europeans also shipped captured Africans to the Americas to replace them. Before this time the captured Africans were shipped to Europe or islands off the coast of Africa.

The Spanish conquerors needed workers for the West Indies and Central America. At first they enslaved the Native Americans to do the work but too many of them died. This created a need for workers from elsewhere.

Captured Africans were shipped directly to the Americas. This became the first leg in a ship's journey. From the Americas, slave produced minerals and foodstuffs were sent to Europe. This was the second leg in a ship's journey. Finally, from Europe, cheap manufactured goods were exported for sale to enslavers in Africa. This was the final leg in a ship's journey.

In the sixteenth century the violence against Africans became more intense in both Africa and Europe. In early November 1570, the Spaniards celebrated the Day of All Saints with the killing of 50,000 Africans living in Spain. In Africa, the Portuguese burned the Swahili cities, invaded Kongo, and invaded Zimbabwe. In the 1590's, the Arabs, with help from England and Spain, destroyed the Songhai Empire.

The Portuguese and Spaniards were the leading slave traders up to the end of the sixteenth century. By the seventeenth century, Holland, England and France took part in the killing of Native Americans and the stealing of their land. They also enslaved Africans and shipped them to the Americas to replace them.

- The Dutch took over Curacao, St Eustatius and Tobago. Also, they ruled New Amsterdam (later called New York)
- The English took over Bermuda (1609) and Barbados (1625). In North America, they conquered Maryland and Virginia
- The French took over Guadeloupe (1626) and Martinique (1635). In North America, they conquered Louisiana
- Finally, the Spanish took over Jamaica and St Augustine in Florida

Source A
Within thirty years of the development of the slave trade, the Portuguese mulattoes [i.e. mixed race] *were in responsible positions as interpreters, brokers, and guards ... Inevitably rape and force were the origins of many of these children ... It is noteworthy how often the secret slaves smuggled on board by members of the crew were women. Almost as quickly as Columbus's sailors spread syphilis in Europe, the crews of the slavers took the disease to Africa.*
(F George Kay, *The Shameful Trade*, 1967)

Source B
I cannot understand why so many Negroes die.
(The King of Spain, *Letter to the Governor of Haiti*, 1510)

ACTIVITIES . . .

1. Make a time line of the important things that happened between 1441 and 1635.

2. How did the Atlantic Age change race relations around the world? What happened to Africans? What happened to Native Americans?

3. Why was it important to build dungeons along the West African coast?

4. According to **Source A**, for what reason might young men from Europe have had for getting involved in the slave trade?

5. Using **Source B** and information on these two pages, outline some of the violent atrocities that Europeans committed against Africans during the Atlantic Age.

LESSON TWELVE: BLACK SOCIETIES IN BRAZIL AND GUYANA

Aim of Lesson: To study the Maroon Societies and the Resistance Movements to Enslavement

The Slave Trade is the history of the Portuguese, Spanish, English, Dutch and French enslavers. It is the history of what these European nations did to Africans. However, Black History in the Atlantic Age is the African rebellions against enslavement. It is also the record of how Africans created Maroon societies.

The Maroons were Africans who ran away and escaped from enslavement. They existed in relatively small communities in North America, Central America, South America and the Caribbean. Some of them revived African traditions, languages and religions. A few of these Maroon societies included Native Americans. The most impressive of these mini-Africas was Palmares, located in Brazil.

In 1595, some enslaved Africans in northern Brazil fled to the forests. They started as a small band of people. The group grew little by little until it became a country of nearly thirty thousand runaway Africans.

They established the first government of free Blacks in the Americas. This was an all Black kingdom in Brazil known as Palmares. Palmares flourished until 1694. King Zumbi was its greatest king. He had a royal guard of 5,000 men. The capital city, Macaco, had a reputation for invincibility. Zumbi had a palace, guards, officials, and royal ceremonies.

Other Maroon communities flourished in the Guyana/Surinam region. The Maroons of Surinam were never conquered.

Source A

Palmares ... ruled an area one-third the size of Portugal. This land was the property of all ... The free Africans planted and harvested a wide variety of products. They also bartered with their white and indigenous Brazilian neighbours. They were very effectively organized, both socially and politically, in their African manner and tradition. They were highly skilled in the art of war. Palmares withstood twenty-seven wars of destruction, waged by both the Portuguese and the Dutch. Palmares resisted for more than half a century: from 1634 to 1694.

(Abdias Do Nascimento, *Brazil: Mixture or Massacre?* 1989)

Source B
Sir Francis Drake's impressions of a Maroon town in Panama

In this town, we saw they lived very civilly and cleanly for as we came near, they washed themselves in the river and changed their clothes which were very fine and well made.

(Sir Francis Drake, 17th Century)

Source C

Dr W E B DuBois provided a list of important rebellions by enslaved Africans that "show that the docility of Negro slaves in America is a myth":

1522	Revolt in San Domingo	1738	Treaty with Maroons
1530	Revolt in Mexico	1763	Black Caribs revolt
1550	Revolt in Peru	1779	Haitians help the United States Revolution
1560	Byano revolt in Central America	1780	French treaty with Maroons
1655	Revolt of 1500 Maroons in Jamaica	1791	Dominican revolt
1663	Land given to Jamaican Maroons	1791-1803	Haitian revolution
1664-1738	Maroons fight British in Jamaica	1794	Cuban revolt
1674	Revolt in Barbados	1794	Dominican revolt
1679	Revolt in Haiti	1795	Maroons revolt
1679-1782	Maroons in Haiti organized	1796	St Lucian revolt
1691	Revolt in Haiti	1816	Barbados revolt
1692	Revolt in Barbados	1828-1837	Revolts in Brazil
1702	Revolt in Barbados	1840-1845	Haiti helps Bolivar
1711	Negroes fight French in Brazil	1844	Cuban revolt

(W E B DuBois, *The World and Africa*, 1947)

ACTIVITIES . . .

1. What is a Maroon Community?

2. List 5 facts about Palmares.

3. What was the greatest achievement of the Maroons of Surinam?

4. Using **Source A**, what evidence is there that Palmares was well organised for military defence?

5. What impression does **Source B** give of the Maroons? What were hygiene levels like in England at this time?

6. According to **Source C**, would it be true to suggest that Africans willingly submitted to enslavement?

LESSON THIRTEEN: BLACK HISTORY IN JAMAICA AND BARBADOS

Aim of Lesson: To study the Maroon Societies and the Resistance

Maroon communities existed in the Caribbean island of Jamaica. The English defeated the Spanish rulers of Jamaica in 1655. The Spaniards fled to Cuba and left their captives to the British. But the enslaved Africans had ideas of their own. They fled to the hills where they fought a war against the English.

Juan de Bolas was the first leader of the Jamaican Maroons. In 1663, after eight years of raiding the English, an attempt was made to get the Maroons on their side. The English made Juan de Bolas a colonel and sent him back to his followers to ask for peace. The Maroons correctly saw this as a trick to re-enslave them. They ambushed their leader and cut him to pieces.

Other groups of escapees flourished elsewhere in Jamaica. The majority of these were originally taken from Ghana. One family shipped to Jamaica soon gained control over the entire Maroon community. The family members were Cudjoe, Accompong, Kofi, Quaco and Johnny.

Cudjoe made his brothers Accompong and Johnny leaders under him. He made Kofi and Quaco subordinate captains. These men led most of the Maroon wars against the English enslavers.

In the end the British were forced to sign a peace treaty with Captain Quaco in 1739. However, the treaty was a backward step. It guaranteed freedom for the Maroons but only on the condition that they returned other escapees to the British. This turned the Maroons into a kind of police force for the British. After the treaty they became an obstacle to the freedom of other Blacks in Jamaica.

In Barbados, the enslaved Africans attempted to take over the entire island on more than one occasion. In 1649 they plotted to kill all the Europeans on the island. However, a treacherous slave revealed the plot. In the end, the English executed eight of the leading plotters.

In 1676 the Africans came up with another plot to take over Barbados. The plotters planned to kill the English and crown Kofi, an enslaved African, ruler of the island. Again, a treacherous slave revealed the plot. The English burned alive six of the leading plotters and beheaded eleven others. Five plotters chose to commit suicide rather than let the English kill them.

Source A

On the east side of the Jamaica, another sizeable group of Maroons formed under the leadership of the legendary Acheampong Nanny. Not much is known of her, but there is a town named in her honour in that point of the island, and her fame has been so great in Jamaican folk tradition that the government has named her the first woman to receive the distinction of National Hero in the year 1975.

(Leonard Barrett, The Rastafarians, 1988)

Source B

The Maroons, in general, speak, like most of the other Negroes in the island, a peculiar dialect of English, corrupted with African words.

(Robert Dallas, The History of the Maroons, 1803)

Source C

Their plan was to have Kofi, a Ghanaian Negro, crowned king ... on an exquisitely made throne. Trumpets to be made of ivory were to be played, with the intention to set fire to the sugar canes and then run in and cut their master's throats. Hearing a young man tell another that he would have no hand in murdering white folk, a house slave informed her master, "thinking it a pity such good people as her master and mistress should be destroyed." The plot was discovered and the ringleaders were caught.

(Contemporary Account in London, 1676)

ACTIVITIES . . .

1. Match the cause to the consequence:

Cause	Consequence
England attacked Jamaica, so	The Spanish left their slaves
The Spaniards could not take their slaves, so	The slaves fled to the Jamaican hills
The British tried to recapture the slaves, so	The British signed a treaty with them
The Maroons would not surrender, so	The Spaniards fled to Cuba

2. How did the Jamaican Maroons become independent in 1655?

3. Why did the British make Juan de Bolas a colonel in the British army?

4. How do you think Juan de Bolas ended up with a Spanish name? Why is this important for Caribbean people today?

5a. Why was the signing of the treaty with the British a backward step for the Maroons?

5b. How might Captain Quaco have justified it to the Maroons?

6. Using **Source A**, for what reasons do you think so little factual information has come down to us about Acheampong Nanny?

7. Read **Source B**. Why do think the Maroons spoke a mixture of English and African languages?

8. According to **Source C** what were the Africans in Barbados planning to do?

LESSON FOURTEEN: BLACK RESISTANCE IN THE US

Aim of Lesson: To study the Maroon Societies and the Resistance Movements in the United States

In the United States, enslaved Africans used various methods to fight against enslavement. They took over slave ships, fought guerrilla wars, and formed military alliances with Native Americans.

There were over 250 armed revolts by Africans against enslavement in the United States. Some of these were joint revolts by Africans and Native Americans.

One of the earliest examples of Africans and Native Americans fighting on the same side against the Europeans was in Hartford, Connecticut in 1657. In the New York City rebellion of 1712, Native Americans fought jointly with Africans. The alliances were due to the two groups being fellow slaves. They both experienced mistreatment by the Europeans. Also they both saw the need to defend themselves from being re-enslaved.

In the United States, some enslaved Africans established Maroon communities of their own. There were at least fifty Maroon communities that existed at various times between 1672 and 1864.

These communities existed in the forest, mountain and swampy regions of several American states: South Carolina, Georgia, Louisiana, Mississippi and Alabama. The most important communities existed in the Dismal Swamp, along the Virginia-North Carolina border. Another important African community existed in Florida in union with the Seminole Indian Nation.

These Maroons tried in varying ways to copy the African societies from which they came. They raised crops and animals. They maintained families with African structures and even traded with the Europeans in certain areas.

Source A

You might be rich as cream
And drive your coach and four horse team
But you can't keep de world from moving around
Nor Nat Turner from gaining ground

And your name it might be Caesar sure
And got your cannon can shoot a mile or more
But you can't keep de world from moving around
Nor Nat Turner from gaining ground

(Folk Song, 19th *Century)*

Source B

The Maroon communities were important for five reasons. Firstly, they showed a possibility of self-rule to other enslaved Africans. Secondly, they helped slaves to escape and reach them. Thirdly, they formed bases from which to launch attacks on plantations. Fourthly, they often raided plantations to free enslaved Africans. Fifthly, they provided leadership and inspiration among the enslaved.

(Maulana Karenga, *Introduction to Black Studies*, 1982)

Source C

Dr Samuel Cartwright of the University of Louisiana thought he had discovered a peculiar disease that only affects Black People. Called Dysthesia Aethiopica, he describes the symptoms a follows:

From the careless movements of the individuals affected with this complaint they are led to do much mischief, which appears as if intentional, but is mostly owing to the stupidness of mind and insensibility of the nerves caused by the disease. Thus they break, waste, and destroy everything they handle; abuse horses and cattle; tear, burn ... their own clothing ... They raise disturbances with their overseers. When forced to work by the compulsive power of the white man, the slave performs the task assigned to him in a careless manner, tredding down with his feet or cutting with his hoe the plants he is supposed to be cultivating; breaking the tools he works with, and destroying everything he touches that can be injured by careless handling.

(Samuel Cartwright, *Dysthesia Aethiopica*, 19th Century)

ACTIVITIES . . .

1. What were the three main methods of resistance that Africans in America used to fight against enslavement?

2. For what reasons did so many of the rebellions also include Native Americans?

3. Where were the Maroon Communities in the United States located?

4. Source A is a praise song for African American rebel leader Nat Turner. Who is it aimed at? What point is the song making?

5. Using **Source B**, explain three reasons why the Maroon Communities were important.

6. Read **Source C**. What do you think Dr Cartwright is REALLY describing here without knowing it?

EXTENDED WRITING

Read **Source C**. Write a spoof article for a medical journal called ***Rebellious Africanus***. Describe the symptoms of this "disease" in some detail.

LESSON FIFTEEN: THE HAITIAN REVOLUTION

Aim of Lesson: To study how the Haitian Revolution helped to end African enslavement

In Haiti, the Africans staged a revolution against the French enslavers. This led to the complete freedom of the Haitian people. Bookman Dutty began the fight on 14 August 1791. He was an African priest and used his religious knowledge to stir the enslaved people against the French.

General Toussaint L'Ouverture continued the revolution against the French. However, the French captured him and starved him to death. Eventually, the revolution against the French was completed in late 1803 under the leadership of Jean-Jacques Dessalines. (See **Image Bank** Figures 13 and 14).

In the battles, the Haitians successfully destroyed two French invasions, a Spanish invasion and an English invasion of their land. After the victory, Dessalines tried and then executed thousands of Europeans for high crimes against the Africans of Haiti. On 22 February 1804, Dessalines gave the orders to execute the criminals. Haiti became an independent country.

One result was that Napoleon, the ruler of France, sold the colony of Louisiana to the United States. Meanwhile, the British got out of the slave trade. In 1807 they passed laws that suppressed the trade. The British and the French did not want a repeat of what went on in Haiti spreading to their other colonies.

Although the slave TRADE was on its way out, enslavement continued for thirty or more years. Enslavement of Africans ended between 1838 and 1888.

Source A
The god of the Europeans inspires him to do crime but our god who is good to us orders us to revenge our wrongs. He will direct our arms and aid us. Throw away the image of the European gods.

(Bookman Dutty, Speech given on 22 August 1791)

Source B
Citizens, it is not enough to have expelled from your country the barbarians who have stained it with blood. It is necessary to ensure the empire of freedom in the country, which has given us birth. Finally, it is necessary to live independent, or die. Independence or Death. Let these sacred words rally us.

(Jean Jacques Dessalines, Speech given on 1 January 1804)

Source C
Another effect of the revolution was the decision by Britain to end the slave trade and the eventual dismantling of the slave system entirely. Actually, abolition was part of a larger plan designed to prevent the Black take-over of the rest of the West Indies and portions of Central and South America. Britain, the United States and other European

powers began secretly supporting white rule to stop the possibility of a repe[...]
Haiti. Indeed, in less than 20 years after the Black nation gained its independen[...]
South America and Mexico became independent under white leadership.

(Jacob Carruthers, *The Irritated Genie*, 198[...])

Source D

Haiti is the glory of the Blacks and the terror of the tyrants.

(David Walker, *The Appeal*, 1829)

Source E

The revolution is one of the noblest, grandest, and most justifiable outbursts against cruel oppression that is recorded on the pages of world history.

(Reverend James Holley, *A Vindication of the Capacity of the Negro Race for Self Government*, 1857).

Source F

We owe much more to Haiti than to them all. I regard her as the original source of freedom of the nineteenth century.

(Frederick Douglass, *Address Dedicating the Haitian Pavilion at the Chicago Exposition*, 1893)

ACTIVITIES . . .

1. Copy this out and fill in the missing words:

The .... led to the end of the .... were worried that if the ......

took over in the ......, they would ...... the Europeans in each island just like in ....

Instead, they stopped the Slave Trade.

Haiti	execute	Haitian Revolution	Caribbean
European enslavers		Slave Trade	Blacks

2. Why did ordinary Haitians follow Bookman Dutty?

3. What did the Europeans do DURING then AFTER the revolution?

4. Read **Source A**. What religion was Bookman Dutty criticising and why?

5. Read **Source C**. Summarise the ideas in 2 sentences.

6. Read **Sources, D, E and F**. How did African Americans, Walker, Holley and Douglas see the Haitian Revolution?

study the most important names in Black Britain in ...nturies

...bers of Black people living in England during the eighteenth
...ries. Some were diplomats from various African countries,
...but most were captives. They worked as household servants,
ta..... ...le, musicians and entertainers.

Ignatius Sancho came to England in 1731 aged two. In later years he wrote musical compositions, poetry and two plays. He married a Caribbean woman and they set up a grocery shop in Westminster. He became a celebrity. The artist Gainsborough painted his portrait. After his death, his letters were published and became a best seller.

Olaudah Equiano was kidnapped with his sister in 1756. He worked as a slave in Virginia and Barbados. A year later he was brought to England but had to work until 1766 to earn enough money to buy his freedom. He became a leader of the African community in Britain. He worked as a miner, hairdresser and a sailor. In 1789, he wrote a book that was very popular called *The Interesting Narrative of the Life of Olaudah Equiano, the African.* He toured Britain and Ireland giving talks at anti-slavery meetings. He also travelled throughout Europe and the Americas. He even voyaged to the Arctic.

Mary Prince was born into captivity in Bermuda in 1788. She was as a children's nurse, a salt miner and a servant. In 1828, she was brought to England. She was continually tortured by her enslavers and chose to run away. She was helped by the anti-slavery society. In 1831 she published a bestselling book called *The History of Mary Prince a West Indian Slave.*

William Cuffay was born in Kent, Enland in 1788. He worked as a tailor. In the 1830s he joined the Chartist movement. They demanded the right to vote for ordinary people. They also demanded rights for workers. Cuffay became one of the leaders of the Chartist movement. In 1848 he was arrested with 11 others and deported to Tasmania. He was pardoned in 1856, but remained in Tasmania where he continued to fight for rights.

Ira Aldridge was an African American actor who came to Britain in 1825. He studied at the University of Glasgow. He also specialised in Shakespeare plays. He toured throughout Britain and Europe. By the 1850s he was established and won many prestigious awards all across Europe. He became the first Black superstar of the Atlantic Age. He died in Poland in 1867 while on tour. (See **Image Bank** Figure 15).

Source A

By the 1770s Britain's Black population may have been 30,000. In London there were large communities in Mile End and Paddington. Black people lived all over the country, especially in the main ports such as Bristol and Liverpool, but also as far afield as Scotland and the Isle of Wight.

(Hakim Adi, *The History of the African and Caribbean Communities in Britain,* 1995)

Source B

Ira Aldridge is the greatest dramatic artist we have ever had. In a little over two years, he has conquered all the sympathies of the public. The critics of Berlin have completely exhausted themselves in praising this lion of the day. His Othello, Macbeth, and Shylock leave him without rival in the history of theatre.

(A German critic on Ira Aldridge)

Source C
An account of the impact Ira Aldridge had in Europe in the 1850s:

King Frederic William IV of Prussia ordered the Gold Medal of Science and the Arts given in his honour. In Austria-Hungary, the Imperial Histrionic Conservatory of Pesch elected him to membership and gave him the Large Gold Medal. In Switzerland, the city of Berne presented him with the Gold Medal of Merit. In Russia, he was a guest of the Czar. The Czar was so impressed that he gave him the First Class Medal of the Arts. In Eastern Russia, the highest honour was conferred on him: Associate of the Order of Nobles.

(J A Rogers, *World's Great Men of Color, Volume II,* 1947)

ACTIVITIES . . .

1. For what reasons were Black people in England? What sorts of jobs did they do?

2. Read paragraphs 2-5. Choose 3 personalities and write 3 facts about each one.

3. In what areas of Britain were Black people most likely to have settled? Which cities have the largest Black populations today?

EXTENDED WRITING

Using **Sources B, C** and paragraph 6, write a letter from the Czar of Russia to Ira Aldridge inviting him to perform in St Petersburg.

Dear Mr Aldridge

Re: Possibility of performing in St Petersburg

We have heard interesting things about you. News reaches us that.....

About you, the critics said ...

We would like to invite you to ...

LESSON SEVENTEEN: THE PAN AFRICAN MOVEMENT

Aim of Lesson: To study the role of Blacks in Britain in the freeing of Africa

The Haitian Revolution showed that European enslavement of Africans could not continue the way it had. By 1888 it was finally over, with millions of Africans deported and millions killed. The death toll from 1441 to 1888 was more than fifty million Africans.

After this the European nations decided to take over Africa and rule it following the 1884-5 Berlin Conference. The Conference involved Great Britain, France, Portugal, Belgium and Germany. The European powers decided to carve up the entire continent between them. This began another tragic chapter in the history of Africans. The Europeans used extreme brutality to seize and rule the conquered lands. At least eleven million Africans disappeared between 1885 and 1900 in the Belgian-controlled Congo.

During this era, Black History emerged in Europe and the Americas. In 1900 Henry Sylvester Williams, a Trinidadian lawyer, called the first of six Pan-African meetings. Held in London, the first Pan-African CONFERENCE interested Black people in England but also had people sailing in from the United States. At the conference, Dr Du Bois, an African American, predicted that the central problem of the twentieth century was going to be "the problem of the colour line".

Dr Du Bois led the first Pan-African CONGRESS in Paris in 1919. At the Congress, the delegates decided to ask the European Colonial powers to protect the Africans that they ruled.

The next three Congresses were equally weak in their demands. At the Second Pan-African Congress in London and Brussels in 1921, the delegates asked that Africans be allowed local self-government. At the Third Pan-African Congress in London and Lisbon in 1923, they asked that "black folk be treated as men". The Fourth Pan-African Congress in New York in 1927 was the last one led directly by Dr Du Bois.

The Honourable Marcus Garvey, Du Bois' rival, tried a different method to get rights for Black people. Born in Jamaica into a Maroon family, he went on to become the greatest Black leader of the twentieth century. (See **Image Bank** Figure 16).

In 1914, he founded the Universal Negro Improvement Associate and the African Communities League. In 1920, the organisation held its first convention in New York. In a short time, the Association had 1,100 branches in more than 40 countries, such as Cuba, Panama, Costa Rica, Ecuador, Venezuela, Ghana, Sierra Leone, Liberia, Namibia and South Africa. Aimed at independence from European rule, the organisation built their own army, the Black Cross nurses, barbershops, bakeries, tailors, newspapers, steamships, and most impressive of all, six million members.

However, by the late 1920s, the Garvey Movement was falling apart. American secret service agents had infiltrated the Association.

Eventually, Mrs Garvey and an ageing Dr Du Bois organised the Fifth Pan-African Congress in Manchester, England in 1945. For the first time, Africans directly from Africa were in large numbers at the event. For the first time the Congress called for African independence. At a much later date … they get it.

The Africans that attended the Conference became major players in the new Africa. Dr Nkrumah, for example, became the first President of independent Ghana in 1957.

Source A

I shall live in the physical or spiritual sense to see the day of Africa's glory. When I am dead wrap the mantle of the Red, Black and Green around me, for in the new life I shall rise with God's grace and blessing to lead millions up the heights of triumph with the colours that you well know. Look for me in the whirlwind or the storm, look for me around you, for with God's grace, I shall come and bring with me countless millions of Black slaves who have died in America and the West Indies and the millions in Africa to aid you in the fight for Liberty, Freedom and Life.

(Marcus Garvey, *Message to the Negroes of the World,* 10 February 1925)

Source B

We support the right of all colonial peoples to control their own destiny. All colonies must be free from foreign control, whether political or economic. The peoples of the colonies must have the right to elect their own Governments, without restrictions from foreign powers. We say to the peoples of the colonies that they must fight for these ends by all means at their disposal.

(*Resolution V from the Pan-African Congress,* Manchester, 1945

ACTIVITIES . . .

1. How many people disappeared during the Slave Trade?

2. What happened in Congo between 1885 and 1900?

3. What was the Pan African Conference in 1900? What did Dr Du Bois mean about the problem of the colour line?

4. What were the UNIA and UCL? What were they attempting to do?

5. Read **Source A**. Why do you think Marcus Garvey was so popular with so many people?

6. Using **Source B** and other information, what was resolved at the Fifth Pan African Congress? Why was it important?

LESSON EIGHTEEN: BLACK LITERATURE IN THE ATLANTIC AGE

Aim of Lesson: To introduce the Black writers from the Atlantic Age

The earliest Black literature outside Africa during the Atlantic Age was the Oral Literature. It was of African origin but with certain changes. The jackal of African oral literature became the fox in the Americas. The hare became the rabbit, the tortoise became the turtle, and the hyena became the wolf. The most popular tales in this literature were the Anansi stories and the Brer Rabbit stories. The Anansi stories were originally of Ghanaian origin where the word "anansi" means spider. The African hare and later rabbit stories in the US are the basis of Walt Disney's *Bugs Bunny* cartoons.

The earliest written Black literature includes the writings of Lucy Terry, Phillis Wheatley, Briton Hamon and Olaudah Equiano. Lucy Terry published a poem called *Bars Fight.* Its subject was the Massachusetts Indian Raid in 1746. After her came the poetess Phillis Wheatley. Briton Hamon wrote a narrative about his life as a slave (1760), as did Olaudah Equiano (1789). Some of these writers were based in the United States, others were in Britain. (See also **Image Bank** Figure 18).

The later writings from the early 1800s were much bolder in condemning the enslavement of Black people as unjust and brutal. George Moses Horton wrote *Hope of Liberty,* James Whitefield published *America and Other Poems,* and Francis Harper wrote *Poems on Miscellaneous Subjects.* The great abolitionist Frederick Douglass wrote an autobiography called *Life and Times.* William Wells Brown and Mary Prince wrote other autobiographical works that called for an end to enslavement.

In 1853 African American William Wells Brown wrote the first Black novel called *Clotel: or the President's Daughter.* In 1857 Frank Webb wrote *The Garies and Their Friends.* This work was famous for its realistic depiction of a race riot. Finally Paul Lawrence Dunbar produced very important poetry in African American dialect. He was the first African American to do so.

Source A

August 'twas the twenty-fifth
Seventeen hundred forty-six
The Indians did in ambush lay
Some very valiant men to slay
The names of whom I'll not leave out
Samuel Allen like a hero fought
And though he was so brave and bold
His face no more shall we behold

(Lucy Terry, *Bars Fight,* 1746)

Source B

I see no reason, but the most deceitful one, of calling the religion of this land Christianity. I look upon it as the boldest of all frauds. We have men-stealers for ministers, women-whippers for missionaries, and cradle-snatchers for church members. The man who wields the blood soaked whip during the week claims to be a minister of Jesus. The man who robs me of my earnings at the end of the week teaches in Sunday School. He who sells my sister for prostitution claims to support moral purity.

(Frederick Douglass, *Narrative on the Life of Frederick Douglass,* 1845)

Source C

Poor Hetty, my fellow slave, was very kind to me, and I used to call her my Aunt; but she led a most miserable life, and her death was hastened by the dreadful punishment she received from my master during her pregnancy. It happened as follows. One of the cows had dragged the rope away from the stake to which Hetty had fastened it, and got loose. My master flew into a terrible rage, and ordered Hetty to be stripped naked, even though pregnant, and tied to a tree. He then beat her as hard as he could till she was streaming with blood. He rested, and then beat her again and again. Her shrieks were terrible. The consequence was that poor Hetty was brought to bed before her time, and delivered a dead child. She appeared to recover but was repeatedly beaten by both master and mistress; but her former strength never returned to her. Her body and limbs swelled to a great size; and she lay on a mat in the kitchen, till the water burst out of her body and she died. All the slaves said that death was a good thing for poor Hetty; but I cried very much for her death.

(Mary Prince, *The History of Mary Prince: A West Indian Slave,* 1831)

ACTIVITIES . . .

1. What is oral literature?

2. How did the oral literature change when enslaved Africans got to the Americas? Give examples.

3. What do **Sources B** and **C** have in common?

4. What problems or difficulties would autobiographies such as **Sources B** and **C** pose for a historian? Explain why the content of such sources make it difficult for historians to stay objective for religious or empathetic reasons.

FURTHER RESEARCH

Use the internet to surf for and read the ***The History of Mary Prince***

LESSON NINETEEN: BLACK SCIENTISTS AND INVENTORS OF THE ATLANTIC AGE

Aim of Lesson: To Study the Black Scientists and Inventors of the Atlantic Age

Benjamin Banneker (1731-1806) was the first of the great Black scientists of the Atlantic Age. He was an inventor, an astronomer, a surveyor and a mathematician. In 1753, he built one of the first wooden clocks in the United States. In 1795, he published an Almanac, which contained (i) an accurate prediction of a solar eclipse, (ii) calculations of the hours of sunrise and sunset for the year (iii) the phases of the moon and (iv) weather predictions. Finally, Banneker was part of a team that planned the layout of Washington DC as it is today. Benjamin Banneker, like most of the important Black scientists and inventors, was from the United States.

Dr George Washington Carver (1860-1943) was the first great Black chemist. He devised methods of extracting or making different products from the peanut, the sweet potato and from pecan. From the peanut, Dr Carver devised 325 different products including cream, buttermilk, coffee, face power, ink, shampoo and vinegar. From the sweet potato, he devised 118 products including flour, starch and rubber. From pecan, he devised 75 products including insulating board, paper, paving blocks and rugs.

Dr Percy Julian (1899-1975) was the pioneering soybean chemist. He invented synthetic cortisone as the first affordable treatment for arthritis. He was also the first to mass-produce male and female hormones. He produced a treatment for the eye disease known as glaucoma. Finally, he invented aero-foam to stop fires.

There were other important African-American scientists. Louis Tompkins Wright became the world's leading thinker on the treatment of aspects of sexually transmitted disease and aspects of cancer. He also invented the neck brace still used today. Dr Charles Drew established the first blood bank in the United States. He was also head of the US and UK blood bank systems during the Second World War.

Jan Matzeliger was the first of the great Black inventors, but unlike the others he was from Suriname of African and Dutch parentage. He produced the first mass produced shoe in 1883. Granville Woods invented the third rail and the overhead conductors for electric trains. He invented a dimmer switch, the telephone transmitter and an egg incubator. Louis Latimer invented the carbon filament for the light bulb. He also supervised the lighting up of New York in 1882 and also London. Garret Morgan invented a gas and smoke mask in 1912 and one of the precursors to the traffic lights in 1923.

Source A

Sir, it is sad to see that although you claim to support the equality of all people, you hold by fraud and violence so many of my brethren under groaning captivity and cruel oppression. You are guilty of the same criminal act that you claim to detest in others.
(Benjamin Banneker, *Letter to Thomas Jefferson,* 1792)

Source B

Arsonists tried to burn down the newly purchased home of Dr Percy Julian to keep him out of Oak Park because he is Negro. We wonder whether these cowards whose mad prejudice drove them to commit this crime would refuse to use the lifesaving discoveries of Dr Julian because they came from the hand and brain of a Negro. Would they refuse to take synthetic cortisone if they were wracked with the pain of arthritis? Would they forbid their wives the use of synthetic female hormone now abundantly available because of Dr Julian's work? Would they refuse to use his synthetic physostigmine if they had the eye disease, glaucoma? If they themselves were caught in a fire, would they order the firemen not to use Dr Julian's great discovery, chemical foam? This stuff saved the lives of thousands of American airmen and sailors during the war.
(*Chicago Sun,* 23 November 1950)

Source C

No Negro blood accepted but –
When the terrible blitz raids of London in September 1940 killed and wounded thousands and an emergency call went out to America for dried blood for transfusions, it was an American Negro surgeon to whom English medical men appealed to organise and send US blood plasma overseas.
No Negro blood accepted but –
When the American Red Cross set up its first blood collection centre in New York for our own armed forces, it was a Negro surgeon who was selected to supervise the entire project and expand the system to every city in the US.
(Chicago Defender, *Negro surgeon World Plasma Expert Derides Red Cross Blood Segregation,* 26 September 1942)

ACTIVITIES . . .

1. List 3 achievements made by Benjamin Banneker, George Carver and Percy Julian

2. Read **Source A**. What impression does this give of Benjamin Banneker? What sort of person was he?

3. Read **Source B**. What can we learn about race relations in the United States from this source?

4. **Source C** is about the fact that blood in the United States was segregated by race. What are the similarities between this source and **Source B**?

43

IMAGE BANK

This part of the book is to provide images necessary to supplement the information.

Figures 1 and 2.
Left: **Pharaoh Mena (ruled 5660-5998 BC). First Dynasty. (Photo: Courtesy of the Petrie Museum of Egyptian Archaeology, University College London, UC 15989).**
Right: **Pharaoh Djoser (ruled 5018-4989 BC). Third Dynasty. (Photo: Courtesy of Wayne Chandler and Gaynell Catherine).**

Figure 3. City of Timbuktu from Henry Barth's *Travels and Discoveries in North and Central Africa,* 1857.

44

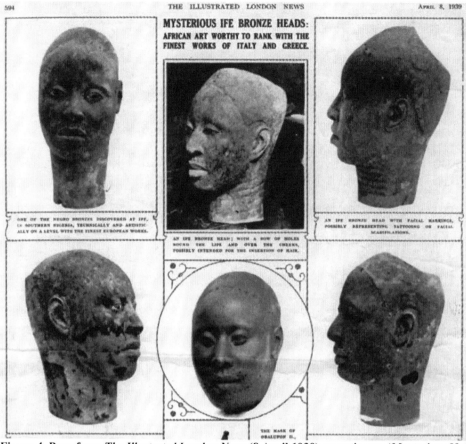

Figure 4. Page from *The Illustrated London News* (8 April 1939) reporting on 'Mysterious Ife Bronze Heads: African art worthy to rank with the finest works of Italy and Greece.' These Yoruba metal masterpieces date from the twelfth to the fifteenth centuries AD.

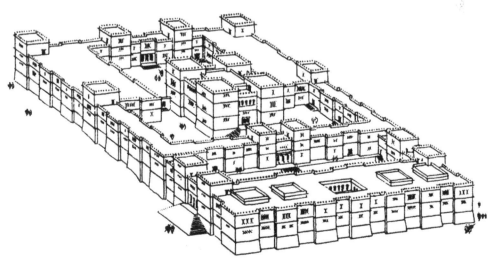

Figure 5. Reconstruction of a castle complex at Axum. *c.*300 AD. The overall dimensions are 80 m x 120 m. From D. Krencker etcetera, *Deutsche Aksum-Expedition, Book II* (Germany, Georg Reimer, 1913, p.113).

Figure 6. View of the Benin capital city during the once yearly procession of the Oba (i.e. King) and dignitaries. Originally published in Olfert Dapper, *Description de l'Afrique*, 1668.

Figure 7. View of the mediaeval city of Lamu, Kenya. Typically Swahili cities had multi storey buildings of up to five storeys. From R. F. Mayer, *Kenya Camera Studies* (Kenya, The East African Standard, 1934, p.24).

Figure 8. Igbo vessel in the shape of a shell surmounted by an animal. 9th or 10th century AD. Leaded bronze. Length 20.6 cm. (Photo: National Commission for Museums and Monuments, Lagos).

Figure 9. Yoruba brass portrait heads discovered near the Palace at Ile-Ife. 12th to 15th centuries AD.

Figure 10. The Great Mosque of Kilwa, Tanzania. Founded in the 10th or 11th century AD, the monument was enlarged in the 13th and 15th centuries. (Photo: Steven D. Nelson, 1993, Courtesy of the Aga Khan Visual Archive, M.I.T.).

Figure 11. Church of Saint George in Lalibela, Ethiopia. Originally published in Susan Denyer, *African Traditional Architecture* (UK, Heinemann, 1978, p.200).

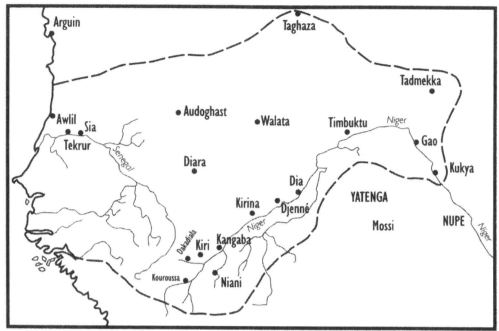

Figure 12. Map of the Empire of Mali.

Figure 13. The aftermath of the Battle for Haiti, as depicted in an old nineteenth century print. The successful conclusion of this battle began the dismantling of the system of mass enslavement of Black people.

49

Figure 14. Jean-Jacques Dessalines (1758-1806) as depicted in an old nineteenth century print. He was the first ruler of an independent Haiti in 1804.

Figure 15. Ira Aldridge.

Figure 16. The Honourable Marcus Garvey (1887-1940). Founder and president of the U.N.I.A. and African Communities League. Consisting of six million people, it was the largest organisation of Black people of all time.

Figure 17. The *Gunda Gunde Gospels*, with superb illustrations and written in the Ethiopic script, 1520. The Armenian and Georgian scripts of Eastern Europe were based on this script.

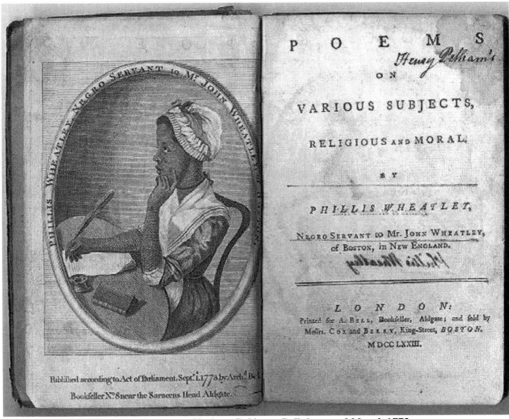

Figure 18. Phillis Wheatley, *Poems on Various Subjects, Religious and Moral*, 1773.

Printed in Great Britain
by Amazon